The Red Wheelbarrow

so much depends
upon

a red wheel
barrow

glazed with rain
water

beside the white
chickens

The Great Figure

Among the rain
and lights
I saw the figure 5
in gold
on a red
firetruck
moving
tense
unheeded
to gong clangs
siren howls
and wheels rumbling
through the dark city.

This is Just to Say

I have eaten
the plums
that were in
the icebox

and which
you were probably
saving
for breakfast

Forgive me
they were delicious
so sweet
and so cold

Metric Figure

There is a bird in the poplars!
It is the sun!
The leaves are little yellow fish
swimming in the river.
The bird skims above them,
day is on his wings.
Phoebus!
It is he that is making
the great gleam among the poplars!
It is his singing
outshines the noise
of leaves clashing in the wind.

in the
much
upon
the
Dreams
they call
Me
Bird
AND
the
Moon
i
This
so
sweet
just
I HAVE
eaten
the

LABOR

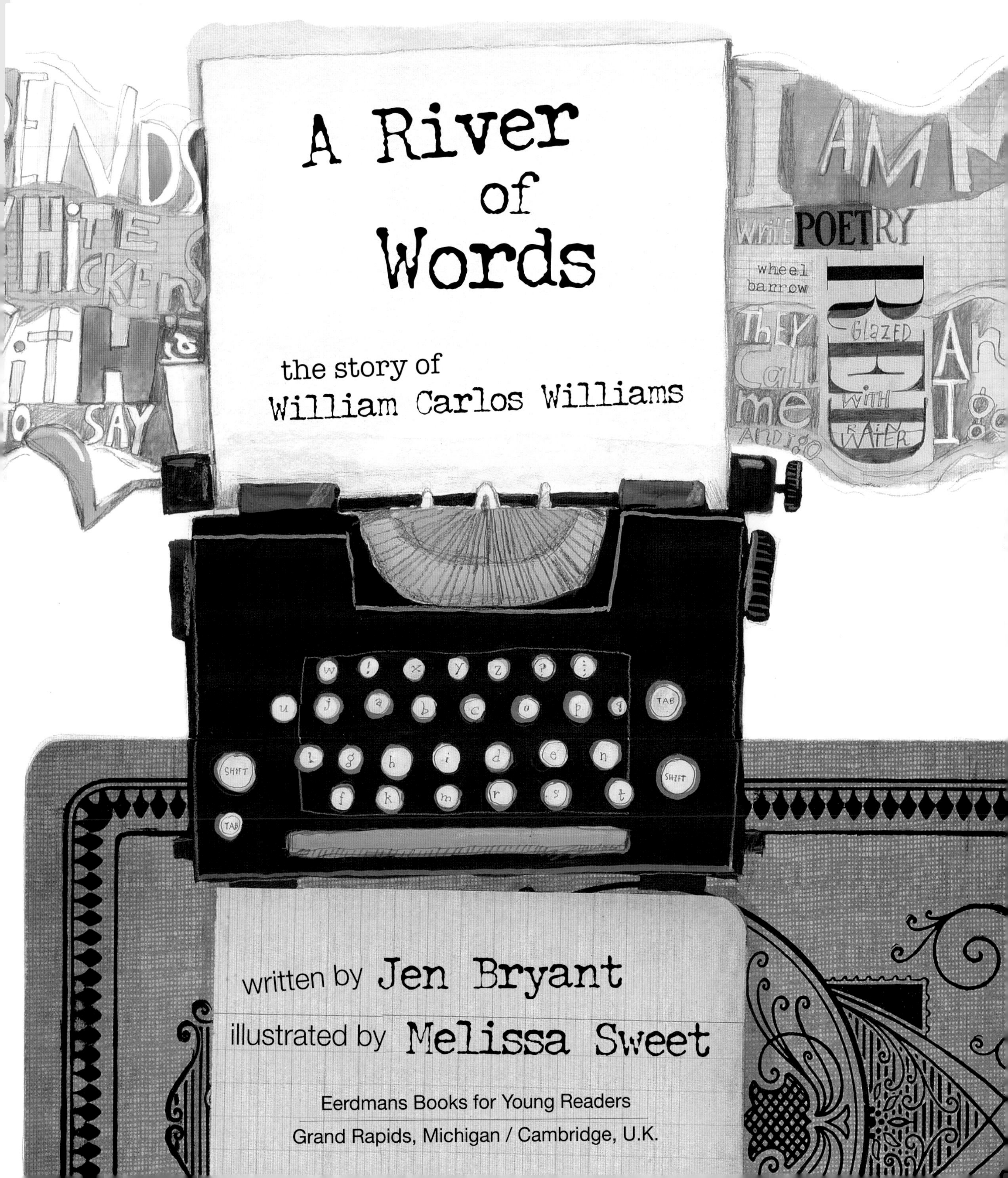
A River
of
Words
the story of
William Carlos Williams
written by Jen Bryant
illustrated by Melissa Sweet
Eerdmans Books for Young Readers
Grand Rapids, Michigan / Cambridge, U.K.
I AM
Write POETRY
wheel
barrow
They
call
me
GLAZED
WITH
RAIN
WATER
SAY

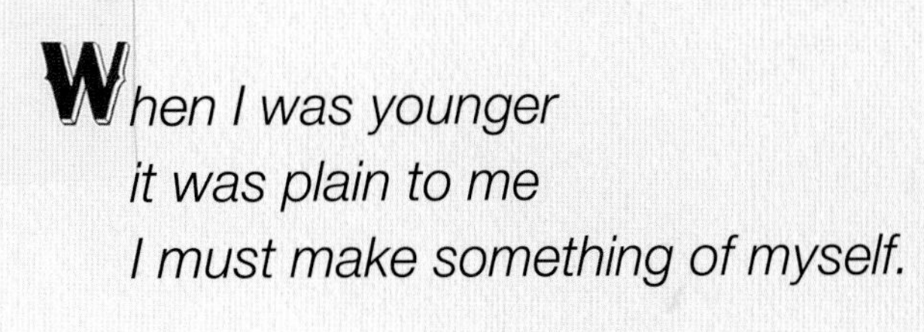

When I was younger
it was plain to me
I must make something of myself.

—William Carlos Williams,
"Pastoral"

Like the other boys in Rutherford, New Jersey,
Willie Williams loved to play baseball
and to race his friends up and down the street.
But when the other boys went inside,

Willie stayed outside. Climbing over the fence
in his backyard, he wandered alone
through the woods and fields.

In those days, just beyond town, there were still many wild places for Willie to explore.
"My Willie has sharp eyes—he notices everything!" his mother told the neighbors. And it was true . . . as he walked through the high grasses and along the soft dirt paths, Willie watched everything.

When he grew tired, he stretched out beside the Passaic River.
Gurgle, gurgle—swish, swish, swoosh!—gurgle, gurgle.

The water went slipping and sliding over
the smooth rocks, then poured in a torrent
over the falls, then quieted again below.
The river's music both excited and soothed Willie.
Sometimes, as he listened to its perfect tune,
he fell asleep.

As Willie grew older, there was less time to wander through the woods and fields or to nap by the river.

In high school, Willie had classes and track practice and lots of homework. "Willie is always in a hurry!" his mother told the neighbors. And it was true.

But when Mr. Abbott read poetry to Willie's English class, Willie did not feel hurried. The gentle sounds and shifting rhythms of the poems were like the music of the river. As the teacher read each line, Willie closed his eyes and let them make pictures in his mind.

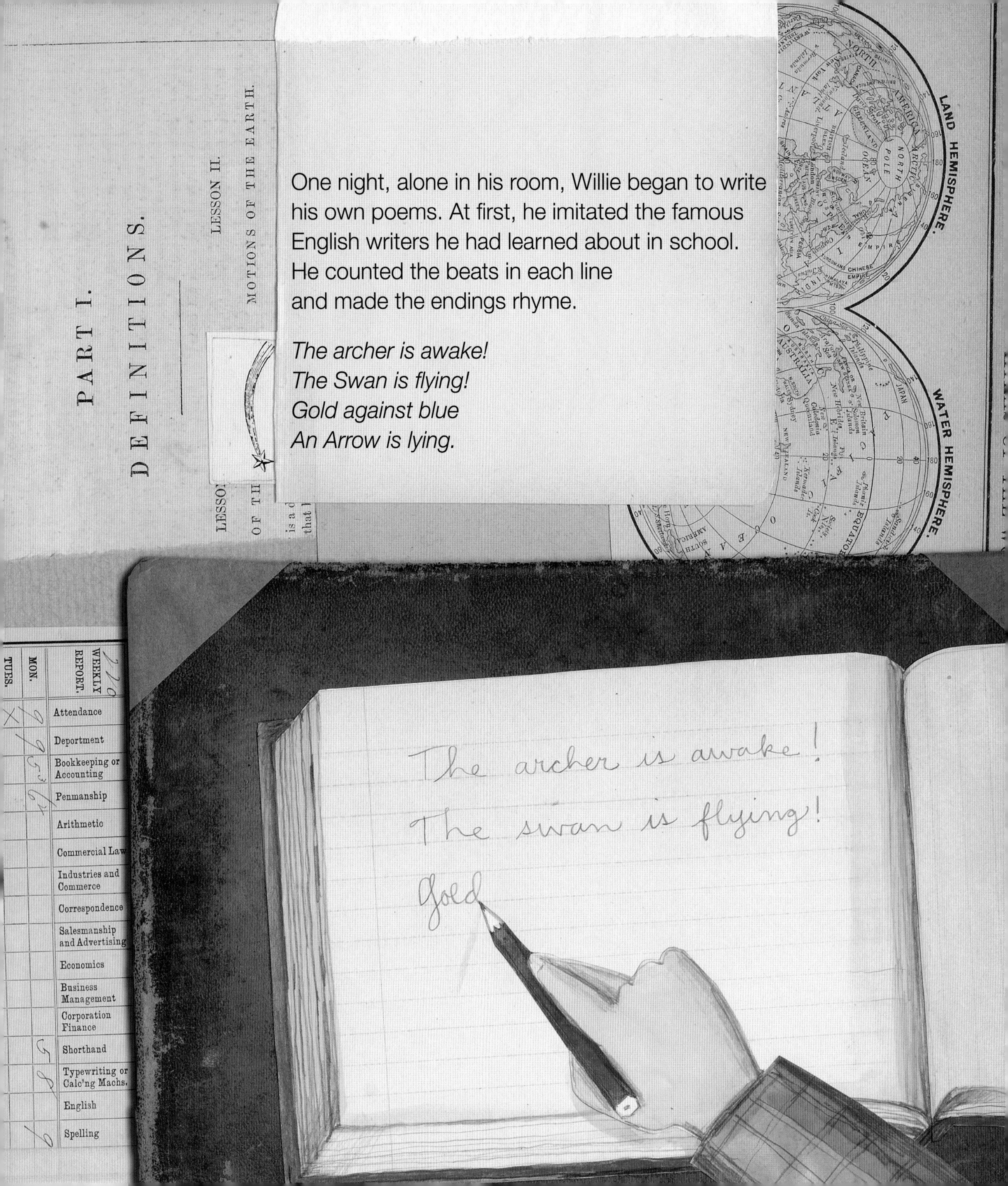

One night, alone in his room, Willie began to write his own poems. At first, he imitated the famous English writers he had learned about in school. He counted the beats in each line and made the endings rhyme.

The archer is awake!
The Swan is flying!
Gold against blue
An Arrow is lying.

Poetry suited Willie. Every night,
he looked forward to sitting at his desk
and writing a few new lines.

But after a while, he grew frustrated.
He had pictures in his mind that didn't fit exactly
into steady rhythms or rhymes.
"I have never seen a swan or an archer," Willie thought.
"I want to write about ordinary things—

plums, wheelbarrows, and weeds,
fire engines, children, and trees—
things I see when I walk down my street
or look out my window."

So Willie tried writing a new way. Instead of
counting the beats or making the end-words rhyme,
he let each poem find its own
special shape on the page.

There is a bird in the poplars!
It is the sun!
The leaves are little yellow fish
swimming in the river.

There is a bird in the poplars!

It is the sun!

The leaves are
little yellow fish
swimming
in the river.

Now when he wrote poems, he felt as free
as the Passaic River as it rushed to the falls.
Willie's notebooks filled up, one after another.

"My boy is a good writer," his mother said. And it was true.
Unfortunately, no one paid much money for poetry,
and Willie needed to earn a living.

The little sparrows hop ingenuously about the pavement quarreling

with sharp voices over things that interest them.

Willie's mother had told him stories about
her older brother, Carlos, who was a doctor.
"When our father died," she told Willie,
"Carlos's salary provided for our whole family."

Willie liked the idea of healing people
and of providing for a family. But could he do both
and still write poetry?

DREAMS

are not a bad thing

I am moved to write poetry

So much depends upon

At age nineteen, Willie went off to study medicine at the university, where he met Ezra Pound, Hilda Doolittle, and Charles Demuth. Ezra and "H.D." were studying literature, while Charlie studied painting.

The friends spent many afternoons together discussing books, music, and art. The harder Willie's medical training became, the more he enjoyed the time he spent with them.

Among the rain
and lights
I saw the figure 5
in gold
on a red
firetruck
moving
tense
unheeded
to gong
clangs
siren
howls
and
wheels rumbling
through the dark city.

Among the
rain and lights
I saw the
figure 5 in gold

FIVE

COLLEGE HISTORIES OF ART

When he graduated,
he returned to Rutherford and hung his sign:
"William C. Williams, M.D.—Family Medicine."

Every morning, Dr. Willie Williams filled his black bag
with medicines and instruments and drove off
to visit patients in their homes.
Every afternoon, he returned to his office
where more patients waited.

6789
rstublwxy
42
890
112
72
ABC
78
45
876
XYZ
TheY CALL ME
AND I GO
TO W. C. WILLIAMS, M. D., DR.
They call me
and I go
FOR PROFESSIONAL SERVICES RENDERED
the door opens
I smile, enter
RECEIVED PAYMENT
24728

All day, he delivered babies, healed hurts and bruises,
set broken bones, and wrote prescriptions
for coughs and fevers.
"Dr. Williams is the busiest man in town,"
said the neighbors. And it was true.

But no matter how many babies he delivered,
no matter how many sick people he cured,
Willie could not stop writing poems.

9 RIDGE ROAD
RUTHERFORD, N. J.

somuchdependsupona
redwheelbarrowglazed
withrainwaterbeside
thewhitechickens

W. C. WILLIAMS M. D.
9 RIDGE ROAD
RUTHERFORD, N. J.

so
much
depends

upon a red wheel barrow
glazed with rain water
water
beside the white chickens
chickens

upon

PROFESSIONAL SERVICES RENDERED

TO W. C. WILLIAMS, M. D., DR.

so much depends

so much depends upon
a red wheel barrow
glazed with rain water
beside the white chickens

d with raine water

rain water
beside the white chickens.

W. C. WILLIAMS M. D.
9 RIDGE ROAD
RUTHERFORD, N. J.

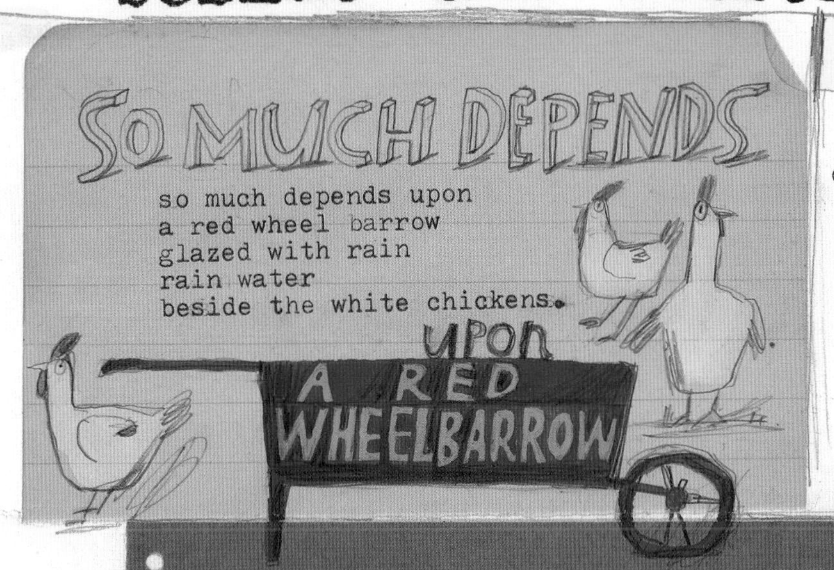

so
much
depends
upon
a
red
wheel
barrow
glazed
with rain
rain
water
beside
the white chickens

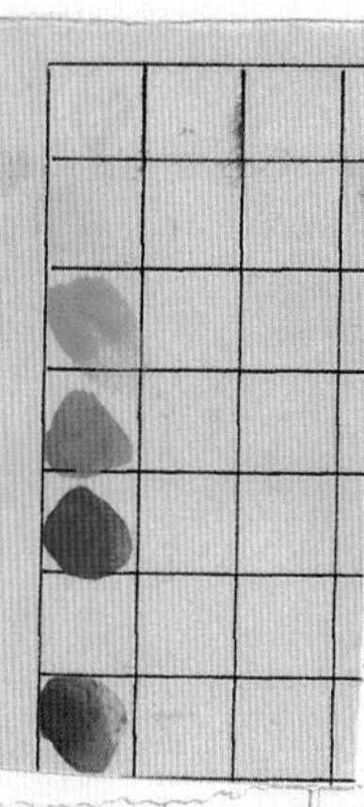

On his prescription pads, he scribbled a few lines
whenever and wherever he could.
In those precious times,
the rhythm of the river he had rested beside
as a child seemed to guide him. Like the water
that sometimes ran slow, smooth, and steady,
and other times came rushing in a hurried flood,
Willie's lines flowed across the page.

After his long doctor's day, Willie climbed to the attic
where he kept a lamp and a desk
filled with letters from his artist friends
and notes he'd made about things he'd heard, seen, or done.

As the rest of Rutherford put out its lights,
Willie took out his pen and his notes.
He sat down and looked at the words . . .

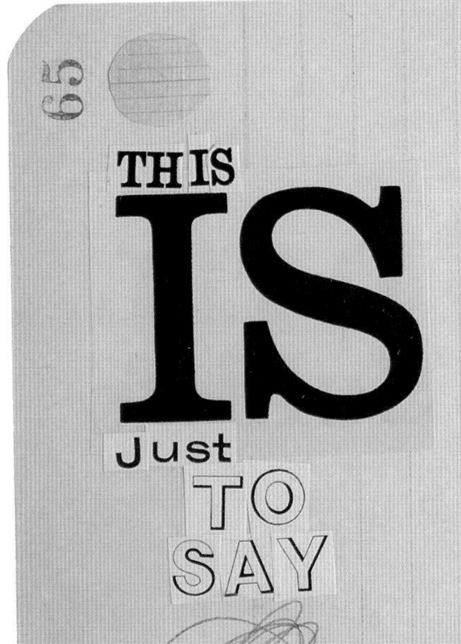
65
THIS
IS
Just
TO
SAY

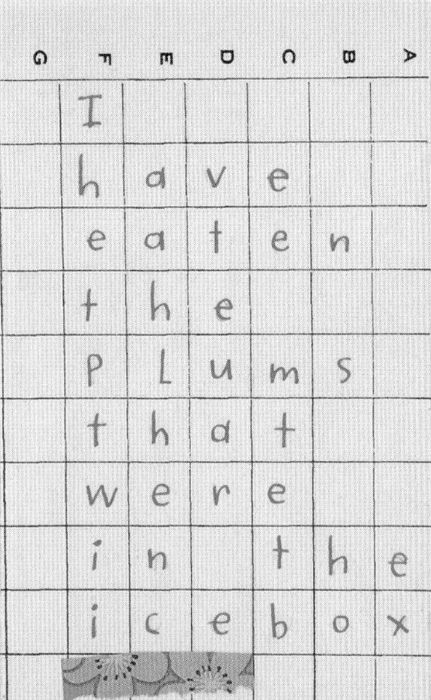
I
have
eaten
the
plums
that
were
in the
icebox

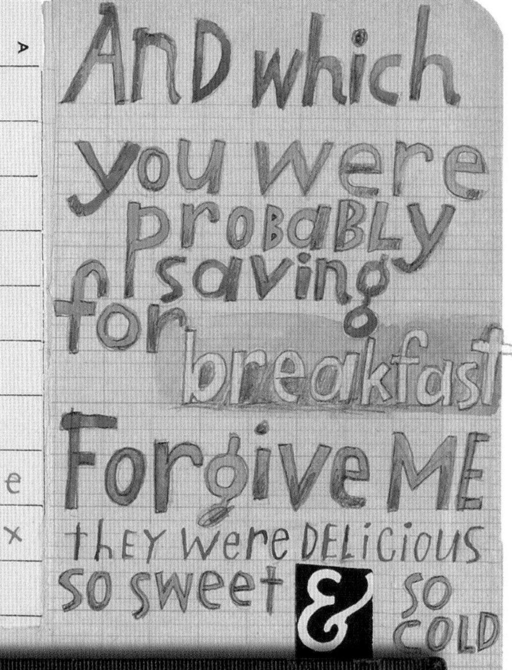
AnD which
you were
probably
saving
for breakfast
Forgive ME
they were DELICIOUS
so sweet & so
COLD

Monday, Aug

. . . and shaped them into poems.

THE MOON

THE DRIED WEEDS

AND THE PLEIADES

SEVEN FEET TALL
THE DARK DRIED WEEDSTALKS
MAKE A PART OF THE NIGHT
A RED LACE
ON A BLUE
MILKY SKY

WRITE
BY A SMALL
LAMP

THE
PLEIADES
ARE
ALMOST
NAMELESS

AND THE
MOON
IS TILTED

AND HALF GONE

William Carlos Williams

1883: (September 17) William Carlos Williams is born in Rutherford, NJ.

1884: Brother Edgar "Ed" Williams is born.

1897–1902: Studies at private schools in Switzerland and France. Attends high school in New York City.

1902: Begins medical school at the University of Pennsylvania in Philadelphia. Makes friends with painter Charles Demuth and poets Ezra Pound and Hilda Doolittle. Writes poetry in his spare time.

1906: Begins three-year medical internship at hospitals in New York City. Continues to write and maintains close friendships with other young artists and poets.

1909: Studies medicine in Germany and travels through Europe. His first verse collection, *Poems,* is printed and published by a friend. It sells only four copies.

1910: Begins his medical practice in Rutherford, NJ, specializing in pediatrics and obstetrics.

1912: Marries Florence "Flossie" Herman.

1913: Purchases a house at Nine Ridge Road in Rutherford, which serves as both his home and his office.

1914: First son, William Eric Williams, is born.

1916: Writes famous poem "The Great Figure," which later becomes the inspiration for Charles Demuth's painting "The Figure 5 in Gold" [1928].

1916: Second son, Paul Herman Williams, is born.

1918: Meets and befriends poet Marianne Moore, who shares Williams's interests in both poetry and science.

Poetry

publication dates

1913
Peace on Earth
"The archer is awake . . ."

1917
Pastoral
"The little sparrows . . . "

1917
Metric Figure
"There is a bird
in the poplars! . . ."

1917
Pastoral
"When I was younger . . ."

World Events

during WCW's time

1886: John Pemberton invents Coca-Cola

1886: Gottlieb Daimler builds the world's first four-wheeled motor vehicle

1901: First radio receiver successfully received radio transmission

1903: Orville and Wilbur Wright fly the first airplane

1907: Color photography invented

1908: First Model T car sold

1910: Talking motion pictures invented

1914: World War I begins

1918: World War I ends

1921
Complaint
"They call me and I go. . . ."

1921
The Great Figure
"among the rain . . ."

1923
The Red Wheelbarrow
"so much depends . . ."

1928
The Descent of Winter
"The moon, the dried weeds . . ."

1934
This is Just to Say
"I have eaten . . ."

1962
The Woodthrush
"fortunate man
it is not to late . . ."

1962
Children's Games II
"Little girls . . ."

1925: Joins the Passaic General Hospital staff but continues in private practice.

1934: Publishes *Collected Poems 1921–1931*. By this time, Williams has published 13 books of poetry and prose.

1935–1945: Continues to create poetry and prose based on everyday scenes and the common working-class experience of his patients. Publishes eight more books of poetry and prose, including *White Mule* and *Life along the Passaic River*.

1946: Publishes first of five books of his epic poem *Paterson*. Others follow in 1948, 1949, 1951, and 1958.

1948: Williams suffers a heart attack. Continues to write but reduces his medical duties. Son William Eric joins his practice.

1950: Receives the National Book Award for his *Selected Poems* and for *Paterson*, Book Three.

1951–1952: Several strokes leave him unable to pursue his medical duties. He recovers well enough to pursue new writing projects and to lecture. Named Consultant in Poetry to the Library of Congress.

1954–1960: Despite fragile health, Williams continues to write. He receives and mentors younger poets at his home, including Robert Creeley, James Wright, Galway Kinnell, Robert Lowell, Allen Ginsberg, and Denise Levertov.

1962: Publishes his 48th book and his last poetry collection, *Pictures from Brueghel*.

1963: (March 4) William Carlos Williams dies at his home in Rutherford. In May, he is posthumously awarded the Pulitzer Prize for *Pictures from Brueghel*.

1927: Charles Lindbergh crosses the Atlantic Ocean non-stop

1929: Stock market crashes

1938: Electronic digital computer invented

1939: World War II begins

1940: Modern color television system invented

1941: US enters WWII

1945: US drops atomic bomb on Hiroshima; WWII ends

1957: Sputnik 1 orbits the Earth

1963: John F. Kennedy, President of the United States, is assassinated.

Author's Note

William Carlos Williams was a family doctor in his hometown of Rutherford, New Jersey, for more than forty years. He specialized in pediatrics (care of children) and obstetrics (delivering babies). Records indicate that he presided over more than 3,000 births. Like most doctors of his time, Williams made house calls, spending his days and some nights, too, caring for the sick in their homes. During the Great Depression, when many adults were unemployed and families could not afford to pay, Williams helped them anyway. Often, after stitching a wound, dispensing medicine for a fever, or helping a woman deliver her child after a long night's labor, he would leave with a homemade scarf, a jar of jam, or a warm casserole as payment.

Despite the constant demands of his profession, Williams always made time for poetry. In his earliest verses, he adopted the methods of traditional English poets who focused on grand topics and used regular patterns of rhyme. Slowly, however, he developed his own distinctive style in which he used shorter lines, brief stanzas, and little or no punctuation. But perhaps his most important contribution to American poetry was his focus on everyday objects and the lives of common people. In his poems, readers can find fire trucks, cats, flowerpots, plums, babies, construction workers, and refrigerators. By stripping away unnecessary details, Williams tried to "see the thing itself . . . with great intensity and perception."

Although he wrote poems for most of his adult life, his poetry was not well known until he was in his sixties. By then, he had already published more than a dozen poetry books as well as several volumes of essays, plays, and short stories. Today William Carlos Williams is considered one of our most influential American poets and his work is read and studied in schools and universities all over the world. Williams died in 1963 at the age of seventy-nine.

—Jen Bryant

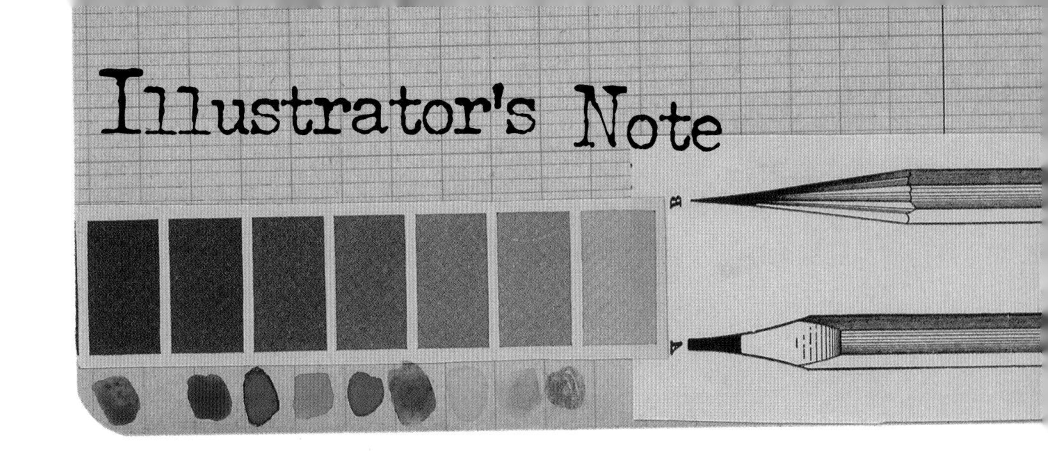

William Carlos Williams's work was inadvertently introduced to me when I was seven years old. Living in northern New Jersey (not too far from where Williams grew up in Rutherford), my Brownie troop took a field trip to the Metropolitan Museum of Art in New York City. My souvenir for that day was a postcard of Charles Demuth's painting, *The Figure 5 in Gold*. What I did not know all those years ago, was that the painting was inspired by a poem William Carlos Williams wrote and shared with Demuth, his longtime friend. Later, even though I had heard the poem, I somehow never connected the two until this manuscript came to me.

The research for this book took me to Rutherford Public Library in Rutherford, New Jersey, where there's a wonderful collection related to Williams's life and work. The librarians there were patient and generous with their time. I want to especially thank Jane Fisher, Director, for showing me photographs, letters, and some of the accoutrements of his life — his desk, typewriter, and straw hat — and for her expertise. I saw Williams's house at 9 Ridge Road, just down the street from the library, and spent time taking pictures and drawing in nearby Paterson, New Jersey.

The artwork for every book calls for a different interpretation. These pictures needed to convey his era and the modern art of his time that was so influential to Williams. There were a lot of false starts—nothing I did seemed powerful enough to match his poems. Then I looked to a big box of discarded books I had from a library sale. One of the books had beautiful endpapers and I did a small painting on it. Then I took a book cover, ripped it off, and painted more. The book covers became my canvas, and any ephemera I had been saving for one day became fodder for the collages.

Every project furthers an artist, but this book was a true gift.

— Melissa Sweet

Baldwin, Neil. *To All Gentleness: William Carlos Williams, The Doctor Poet*. NY: Atheneum, 1984. (foreword by Wm. Eric Williams, MD)

Bloom, Harold. *William Carlos Williams*. Bloom's Major Poets Series. Chelsea House, 2002.

The Collected Poems of William Carlos Williams, Vol. 1: 1909–1939, Litz, A. Walton & Christopher MacGowan, ed. NY: New Directions, 1986.

The Collected Poems of William Carlos Williams, Vol. 2: 1939–1962, MacGowan, Christopher, ed. NY: New Directions, 1991.

Poetry for Young People: William Carlos Williams. MacGowan, Christopher, ed. NY: Sterling Publishing Company, Inc., 2003.

Pratt, William. *The Imagist Poem: Modern Poetry in Miniature*, rev. ed. Ashland, OR: Story Line Press, 2001.

William Carlos Williams: Selected Poems. Pinsky, Robert, ed. NY: Library of America, 2004.

William Carlos Williams — Voices & Visions. WinStar TV & Video Productions, VHS. 1999.

www.poetryfoundation.org/programs/children.html/archive

www.poets.org/poet.php/prmPID/119

For Leigh and Zinta

—*J.B.*

For Lisa

—*M.S.*

Published in 2008 by Eerdmans Books for Young Readers
an imprint of Wm. B. Eerdmans Publishing Co.

Wm. B. Eerdmans Publishing Co.
Grand Rapids, Michigan

www.eerdmans.com/youngreaders

Manufactured in China

25 24 23 22 21 20 19 16 17 18 19 20 21 22

Library of Congress Cataloging-in-Publication Data

Bryant, Jennifer.
A river of words / by Jen Bryant ; illustrated by Melissa Sweet.
p. cm.
This picture book biography of William Carlos Williams traces childhood events that lead him to become a doctor and a poet.
ISBN 978-0-8028-5302-8 (alk. paper)
1. Williams, William Carlos, 1883-1963—Childhood and youth—Juvenile literature. 2. Poets, American—20th century—Biography—Juvenile literature. 3. Physicians—United States—Biography—Juvenile literature. I. Sweet, Melissa, ill. II. Title.
PS3545.I544Z5823 2008
811'.52--dc22
[B] 2007049347

Display type set in John Doe
Text type set in Helvetica Neue
Illustrations created with watercolor, collage, and mixed media.

Timeline photograph by Irving Wellcome, courtesy of New Directions Publishing

Selected poems by William Carlos Williams, from *Collected Poems: 1909-1939*, Volume 1,

Quotations from W.C.W. and his friends:

William Carlos Williams, poem, A Sort of Song, c.1944 in *The Collected Poems of William Carlos Williams* Volume II, 1939-1962, Edited by Christopher MacGowan (New Directions Publishing, 1988). website: poetryfoundation.org/archive/feature.html

Hilda Doolittle, poem, Sheltered Garden, H.D. Collected Poems, 1912-1944 (New Directions Publishing, 1986). website:poetryfoundation.org/archive/poem.html <http://www.poetryfoundation.org/archive/poem.html?id=177770>

Charles Demuth, article, "Across A Greco is Written" from Creative Art, September, 1929. website: demuth.org/Vol16NO33.htm#Creative%20Arts

Ezra Pound, essay, "I gather the Limbs of Osiris" from Selected Prose, edited by William Cookson (New Directions Publishing, 1975).

Pastoral

The little sparrows
hop ingenuously
about the pavement
quarreling
with sharp voices
over those things
that interest them.
But we who are wiser
shut ourselves in
on either hand
and no one knows
whether we think good
or evil.
Meanwhile,
the old man who goes about
gathering dog-lime
walks in the gutter
without looking up
and his tread
is more majestic than
that of the Episcopal minister
approaching the pulpit
of a Sunday.
These things
astonish me beyond words.

Children's Games II

(Part X, pictures from Brueghel)

Little girls
whirling their skirts about
until they stand out flat

tops pinwheels
to run in the wind with
or a toy in 3 tiers to spin

with a piece
of twine to make it go
blindman's-buff follow the

leader stilts
high and low tipcat jacks
bowls hanging by the knees

standing on your head
run the gauntlet
a dozen on their backs

feet together kicking
through which a boy must pass
roll the hoop or a

construction
made of bricks
some mason has abandoned